AUSTRALIA AT WAR

A Winter Record on the Somme and at the Ypres
During the Campaigns of 1916 and 1917

Will Dyson

DEDICATED
TO THE MEN OF THE A.I.F.

To you who tread that dire itinerary
Who go like pedlars down the routes of Death,
Grey in its bloody traffic, but who gaze
Inured upon its scarlet merchandise
With eyes too young to have yet wholly shed
The pity moving roundness of the child—
To you, like cave men rough-hewn of the mud,
Housed in a world made primal mud again,
With terrors of that legendary past,
Reborn to iron palpability,
Roaring upon the earth with every wind—
To you who go to do the work of wolves
Burdened like mules, and bandying with Death—
To hide the silent places of the soul—
The ribald jests that half convince the blind
It does not wholly anguish you to die—
To you who through those days upon the Somme,
About you still the odours of our bush,
I saw come down, with eyes like tired mares,
Along the jamming traffic of Mametz,
Creeping each man, detached among his kind,
Along a separate Hell of memory—
To you, and you, I dedicate these things
That have no merit save that they, for you,
Were woven with what truth there was in me
Where you went up, with Death athwart the wind
Poised like a hawk a-strike—to save the world,
Or else to succour poor old bloody Bill

Beleaguered in a shell hole on the ridge.

W. D.

Table of Contents

Artist's Note
Introduction
Bringing up the Stew
Reporting at the Battery
Dead Beat
The Cook
Group
Looking for the Battalion
The Mate
Tunnellers under German Territory
Coming out on the Somme
Labour Battalion Man
Back to the Waggon Lines after Polygon Wood
Lightly Wounded at a Menin Road Dressing Station
Stretcher-bearers near Martinpuich
"Waiting for the Stew"
In the Tunnel—Hill 60
Fatalist
Outside the Pill Box
Coming out at Hill 60
"Hanging About"
Down from the Ridge

Artist's Note

This selection of drawings, made during the winters at Ypres and on the Somme reflects more the misery and the depression of the material conditions of these campaigns than it does any of their exaltations or their cheerfulnesses.

Here and now—here on the new Somme and now when Spring is about us in a land upon which War has not had time to fully wreak his wicked will—these two latter qualities are dominant. In the spirit of Dernancourt and of Villers-Bretonneux the selection made from my drawings may seem to overstress this winter note. They are not primarily cheerful—but it is open to doubt whether we are behaving generously in demanding that the soldier who is saving the world for us should provide us with a fund of light entertainment while doing it.

The truth is that War has many moods and nothing more is hoped than that the selection made from my drawings and my notes may record something of the one of its moods to which I was temperamentally most attuned during those bad seasons on the Somme and at Ypres.

W. D.,

France,
May, 1918.

Introduction

EVERYBODY knows that Mr. Dyson, who has made these striking sketches of the great war in which he has himself been wounded, originally became famous as a caricaturist, probably the most original caricaturist of our time. To some it may even need a word of further explanation adequately to connect a caricaturist so fanciful with a tragedy so grave and grim. Nor indeed is the connection only that more obvious one, which has drawn so many men of genius into duties that are simply normal because they are national. Mr. Dyson is indeed as patriotic in external as he is public spirited in internal politics; but his case here must not be confused with what might have occurred if, in some national crisis, the late Phil May had drawn a cartoon for Sir John Tenniel, or if the late Dan Leno had sung, with all possible sincerity, a patriotic song. In such cases men might say that great artists were behaving like good citizens; but that it was rather of their ordinary than their extraordinary qualities that they were at that moment justly proud. The importance of Mr. Dyson's work cannot be properly appreciated unless we realise that his patriotism and public spirit are extraordinary as well as ordinary; for to be extraordinary without being also ordinary is merely another name for being mad. Mr. Dyson in becoming more national does not become less individual; nor does he for the first time become serious. The graver work of such an artist will not be merely grotesque, if only because his most grotesque work was always full of gravity. His caricature was a criticism, and indeed a very severe criticism, of the whole modern world. And it is perhaps the severest of all criticisms on the modern world, that the one form of art that has rendered it most seriously and most subtly, is the art of caricature. Here it may well be left an open question whether this character in our time, as compared with former times, means that we more easily appreciate satirists, or merely that we more easily lend ourselves to satire.

In any case the lightest, wildest or even crudest sketch scratched down by Dyson has always had more of the true grip of gravity than the whole of the Royal Academy. It is our modern misfortune that what is most solemn is most frivolous; because it is, in motive if not in method, most facile. There is always genuine thought in the design as well as the detail of Mr. Dyson's work; and it is thought of a kind that is too little defined or understood. Where he has always differed from a common capable caricaturist is approximately in this; that it was never the comic but rather the serious feature that he caricatured. It is the soul rather than the body that he has drawn out in long fantastic lines. His comedy has never been merely comic, but rather philosophic and poetic. When he drew a Jew he did not merely draw the nose of a Jew, as a man might draw the trunk of an elephant; the most prominent thing about an elephant but not the most elephantine. He would rather draw that oriental type of eye, so strange in its shape and setting; which can be seen carved on colossal Assyrian masks of stone or painted flat on the cases of Egyptian mummies. And this marks his philosophic sentiment; he throws on things a new light which is also an ancient light; which is in its nature historic and even pre-historic. This is what links him up with the school of the great satirists; for it is one of the chief strokes of satire to tell new things that they are old; nay, in a sense to extinguish them by telling them they are eternal. But there is necessarily the same sort of epic symbolism underlying his treatment of the toils and perils he most sincerely admires, as underlying his treatment of the luxury and tyranny he has most drastically denounced or exposed. And that is why something of this almost allegoric spirit must be appreciated, in appreciating his studies of the appalling pageant of the great war.

Being a satirist he is a humorist; but we must not look for mere lively notes of what may be called the humours of the trenches. Nothing can be more admirable in another aspect than those humours; or above all than the humour, and especially the good humour, which generally endures and records them. But such an artist is not concerned so much with that comic relief, by which details are relieved against tragedy, as with that high and tragic relief by which the tragedy itself is relieved against the light of heaven. Indeed there is something significant in all that white light and sharp shadow which belongs to such scenes, and is so favourable to the art of black and white. There is even something of allegory in that awful and empty daylight in which armies live, so often without a stick of roof or a rag of curtain. All the soldiers in a great war are historical characters; but these are rather specially standing, not against court or camp, but only against the sky. They are under a light which will indeed prove eternal; even as compared with other historic groups they will continue in a sort of permanent publicity; for we do not yet realise from what distant heights and terraces of time the arena of this war will be seen. And therefore it is, perhaps, that through all the rags and rude equipment that Dyson draws can be traced the lines of a sort of nakedness, like that of the dead on the Last Day.

It may be that such a criticism is too much haunted by the shadow of those sharp satiric and philosophic designs of his former work; in which the draughtsmanship was itself a kind of swordsmanship. But those who have most valued his more fantastic visions will be disposed to recognise this larger reality through the veil of realism. They will be able to see the old and true types of mankind, as it were, in a masquerade of khaki. A certain loose precision of line, which renders the length of limb or the lightness of the lifted head in the young soldier, is the same as that which gave, in the Labour Cartoons, a new and too much neglected dignity to the young workman. And it will be well to note this; since a conventional patriotism is too prone to forget that the young soldier generally is the young workman. But neither in the new sketches nor the old ones was the dignity merely dignified, in the sentimental manner; and many will still think it comic precisely because it is tragic. In this sense there is a note of satire in the names of famous or notorious London streets, stuck up as labels in the tunnels of the sunken labyrinth of trench warfare. It is wholesome to remember that many of these men have sat or stood with as haggard an endurance upon the stones of the real streets at home; and have suffered almost as much from the horrors of peace as from the horrors of war. Nor should we forget how much of the life of labour has been subterranean, and with less hope of an outlet on victory. Tyranny is in a true sense oppression; it is the weight of worldly evil that the artist has felt; a thing not so much unearthly as unnaturally earthly. And this again will always make him a true interpreter of the great war, whether in the idealism of caricature or the realism of such work as this. For what the free men of the world are now labouring to lift is indeed an oppression almost in the literal sense of a load; it is like a nightmare in this vital sense, that while it lasts it seems, not less, but more real than reality. The barbarism which all free men defy to-day might well be embodied in one of the Dyson demons, swinish, swollen, sullen; the thing described by the genius of an artist in another art; by M. Emile Cammaerts writing also of the Satan who has set up his throne in Belgium:

"*Il n'est pas triste; il n'est pas fier; il n'est pas beau;*

Il n'est pas même troublant; il n'est pas ambigu;
Il est laid; il est lâche; est gros, il est sot;
Et il pue!"

    We are fighting against a living slime, like that mud of Flanders which men loathe more than wounds and death. And indeed the two spirits of the war might be conceived as meeting in the flats of the Flemish coast under the emblems of the two elements; the strange slow strength of the inland swamp and the force and freedom of the sea. Against such elemental emptiness of bare lands and bleak waters. Dyson has moved and showed his comrades moving; and his stroke is here none the less militant because he is now using only the artillery of art, which fights not with fire but with light.

G. K. CHESTERTON

Bringing up the Stew

". . . . The precious fluid, the hope-giving potion, the stew from the wagon lines, the last evidence of the existence on earth of any civilization or culture that the battalion will know for some days. It was to be a real stew with fresh meat, and in this case it was a triumph of the art, something to send the boys from supports into the line if not singing the merry songs of the imaginative press at least with some of the content of the gorged python. . . . .

"When the look-out saw the panting carriers coming over that greasy mixture of mud and water and desolation known as Flanders, they raised the equivalent of a cheer and hope again raised her drooping pennons. You have got to die—don't die hungry if you can help it. To have fluked a good meal before you go is to have cheated death to the extent of having bagged a good human satisfaction under his chagrined nose. And that is so much to the good.

. . . . an article of importance in the credo of that narrow land that runs from Nieuport to the Alps—where things are as they were and things are valued as they were in the deplorable beginning of all things."

Reporting at the Battery

".... H——'s two men had floundered back to the guns from the forward Observation Post after this very thick night and reported to 'M——.'

"'M——' was very liberal to them with Hurley's whiskey—and they needed it. This sort of need for a drink is something that bears no relationship to anything you and I could ever know in a nicely regulated civilian life. It is of a world which the temperance die-hard has never envisaged, and in which the drink does nothing more criminal than make man more stoical of conditions that in themselves are cruel enough to justify him in committing the seven cardinal sins if that would procure alleviation of those conditions."

Dead Beat

"He was there as we came back with Wilkins after watching the reply to the S.O.S., sleeping on the eternal petrol tin, and was there when we got breakfast—dead to the world . . . . I have not at all drawn him as childish as he looked . . . . He had come down with a relief from somewhere near Glencorse Wood and had lost himself and floundered all night in shell holes and mud through the awful rain and wind which seemed to have power to wash out the very gunfire of Manton's battery. He had floundered into the cover of the tunnel and stopped there, disregarded, save for occasional attempts to assist on the part of the men—attempts that could not penetrate through to his consciousness past the dominating instinct to sleep anywhere, anyhow, and at any cost . . . . The boys tried to get him to report to the Pommy Colonel in another gallery . . . . but he dropped off again into that coma of a spent man, too spent to be wholly unconscious of his misery even in sleep . . . . and I heard him muttering in a sullen diminuendo, like a rebellious schoolboy, 'Bloody war!! Bloody war!! Bloody war.' . . . . He looked like the hundred others one has seen—like many in the company that were lining the corridors, but that his abandonment was greater—he was emphatically lost, lost like a child, and evoking some of the pity that goes to a child, he looked so very young—that quality which here has power to touch the heart of older men in the strongest way. To see going into the line boys whose ingenuous faces recall something of your own boyhood—something of someone you stole fruit with, or fought with or wagged it with through long hot Australian afternoons—to see them in this bloody game and to feel that their mother's milk is not yet dry upon their mouths . . . ."

The Cook

".... who is at his noblest when he has graduated in the shearers' sheds. I speak not as a gourmand of the table. I sometimes think it is the primitive emotions of grief and disillusionment and ferocious despair induced by the cooking of the cooks that make some of our battalions so awe inspiring in the attack.

"No, this superiority indicated is not so much from the point of view of cooking as of character. The cook stands apart in his little niche of fame. He has with him the democracy of the shearer's shed, coloured with the exclusiveness of the artist, the practitioner of mysteries. The work of the Divine Sculptor as it came from His chisel, rough hewn as the Master left it. What he was he will be.

"The cook stands apart in his little niche of fame eternal and unchangeable, as God and the democracy of the shearing shed made him. The Army and its War Councils, its Field Marshals, its G.S.O.'s, its N.C.O.'s, retire foiled and chagrined in their puny efforts to unmake what these two have made. . . . It is with a mixture of the two qualities—the equality of the shearing shed and the exclusiveness of the studio—that he meets them all, from Brigadiers to Batmen. A manner that frankly accepts the doctrine of the brotherhood of man with its implied admission that after all he is no better than the Colonel. . . . Yes, his cooking may be bad but his heart is good. As Mac used to sing:

"''E aint't no Anzac 'ero who gets 'is photo took,
'E is greasy but a white man is the old Battalion Cook.'

"I have often suspected that Australian units select their cooks not on their ability as chefs but for the stories that can be told about them to other units. It is a sort of competition, and the cook who said, 'I know I'm no chef from the 'otel Australia, but there ain't a willinger cook on the Somme!' was worth it, cooked he ever so badly. He often has, or had, a son or two in the line who probably left Australia criminally young to prove themselves men as the old man left to prove himself one of the boys. And in moments of depression, to which he is liable, he is full of mutinous threats of his intention to get back to the line again where the men are. . . ."

Group

"I started to do a drawing for a Christmas Card for the battalion, representing some of the boys thinking of Australian summer, in the mud of this Flanders winter, but the thing was a little too funereal to force on fighting men. I did them one dwelling more on the light and gamesome aspects of a life of slush, sandbags, shells and sacrifice. . . . The passion of soldiers for amusing drawings of the front is a different thing to the civilians demand for them. . . . . It is a proper and wise attitude for the soldier to take towards his hardships, but for the others to be so preoccupied with discovering the humours of the soldier's lot is scarcely seemly."

Looking for the Battalion

". . . . On the road . . . . the incongruities of the traffic—the ammunition carrier down from the guns with his mule covered with mud and himself disreputable to a point beyond the dreams of any civil tramp—a thing I am sure countless irreproachable patriots at home would imprison on sight—breathing grim blasphemy and jostled by staff cars polished and hermetically sealed against the blast that affect the men of mortal clay. . . . the labour battalion man with those characteristics especially and irrevocably his—the Chinese with his invincible good humour and horse play. . . .

"The foot traffic, the men coming and going from divisional baths, bearing towels, coming from and going to that area where are estaminets, those links with a civilian past—those fairy lands within the four walls of which we can behave almost with the godlike freedom of the aristocratic days when one was a vendor of vegetables, a server of writs, a pleader of causes, a duke or a dustman.

". . . . The men who are seeking their battalion—who drift out of nowhere, asking the whereabouts of the 27th, or the 10th, or the 6th, and who drift on into nowhere, and no doubt ultimately find there what they seek—no doubt through the exercise of a native scepticism regarding what is told them. For as there is a lot of human nature in war and it is human to wish to impart information, information is imparted with more willingness than accuracy, here even more than elsewhere. No doubt they find it, for all things are ultimately found in the army, through the Chinese patience with which the life has imbued all—a patient and an oriental sense of the unimportance of time bred by countless experiences which tells you that however long it takes you to get there you will one day or one year get there without disaster, and to hurry it unduly is bad in philosophy and unavailing in fact . . . .

"They come, these strays, from leave, from all those temporary detachments from their units, from hospital, from rest camps, and they live on the country, trusting no doubt to the freemasonry, the trades' unionism of the fighting man, the large confederation—the offensive and defensive alliance of the lance-privates.

"From rail heads and the tender mercies of R.T.O.'s, they move over France through villages, and over what were villages—over duck boards and shell holes with that grousing league-devouring indifference to all things made which is bred by a life two-thirds of the activity of which is moving from a place you don't want to be in to a place you don't want to go to."

The Mate

"Most of the boys are of that age at which friendship is not the tepid give and take of years of discretion. Remember our friendship at twenty! At that age a friendship is a thing intense and unquestioning—it is blasphemy to it to think of it as anything less than eternal. . . . . Normally those friendships wither painlessly in their season, but this generation, or what maimed fragment of it lives through it all, will live with the memory of heroic friendships cut off at the height of their boyish splendour, and which can never suffer the slow deterioration of disillusionment.

. . . You see what an invitation to grief is friendship with the regiments of foot. . . . They are touchingly profane about the dead friend . . . . They see that a cross comes from the battalion carpenter, or the especial friend like little 'W——' makes a cross himself and carves an ornate rising sun on it—but they are movingly profane about it all, employing all those proper expedients of the Digger for the disguising of deep feeling—of the exhibition of which the boys are so timid that they have evolved a language compound of blasphemy and catch phrases in which they can unpack their hearts without seeming to be guilty of the weakness of emotion."

Tunnellers under German Territory

"The tunneller's activity is only heard of when the world is deafened by the blowing of a mine that he has prepared through months of silent, modest and retiring labour; labour that in its nature is coy and shy of observation. A form of warfare with its stratagems and incredible counter stratagems . . . for which the Australian miner has peculiar advantages . . . . to these strange places he brings all that was characteristic of him in the Lady Berry at home . . . .

"It was our tunnellers who prepared a little show which an English battalion carried out, and the night of the touch off a battalion commander said to a tunnelling officer, 'I think I should tell you that I am given to understand that some of your men are going to attempt to go over with us to-night.' Which it is understood that the tunnellers did contrive to do, for the next day a tunneller showed 'P——' a fine Fritz watch. 'You don't get them tunnelling, sir,' he said. 'The infantry will do me after this.'"

Coming out on the Somme

". . . . The haunting memory of the Somme, those ghosts of young men treading their pale way through the substantial virility of its wheel-choked arteries . . . . moving like chain gangs dragging invisible chains.

"They came back, these pioneers of the liberties of the world, with them still the eternal mystery of no man's land, men walking in their sleep . . . . young men bearded like unshorn Andalusians, and garbed like ragged adventurers of another age . . . . companions of a new Marco Polo returned from gazing on strange and terrible lands."

Labour Battalion Man

"He looks so like a fragment of civilian England, strayed incongruously into these warlike areas. One might say he smells of the comic paper, of the Music Hall, of the comic British workingman, were it not that there is a twist in the humour of it all that moves to other things than happy laughter . . . .

"It is a sorry jest that they, these unfit, the delvers of the earth, simple and twisted labourers with a Saxon faith in beer, should be the material in which war and the very great work out their soaring ambitions. . . . . But I am sometimes solaced by the feeling that their miseries are not very much grosser than those in which a grateful country found them when war made her cognisant of their civic existence."

Back to the Waggon Lines after Polygon Wood

"The quarter-master had spent a feverish day gathering what comforts he could for the returning braves, fussing about like a good housewife expecting the return of her lord. Begging and borrowing and by less legitimate means accumulating those things that would make it something of a home-coming—the return to this spot—desolate and shell shriven by the shells of three years and the bombs of last night, but at the worst a haven of effeminate ease to the home-comers.

"The cooks had worked with an energy that is explained by the fact that love and kindness are best expressed in the primitive world by food and, sentimental though it sounds, they wanted to show both of those things. Those profane slushies were the representatives of that fundamental and admirable human instinct to comfort the stricken with food, to gorge the tired hero.

"The strays began to arrive alter midnight, in ones and twos and threes, directed by the battalion guides posted on the route, and from then onward the groups thickened and dispersed and gathered again around the cookers that shone like lode stars in the gloom. They came down the road out of the night asking for A company, B company, C company, leaning well forward to balance the light pack on the shoulders, the silent, the garrulous, the boisterous and the grim, and presenting their dixies for stew on the right, tea on the left. . . .

". . . all with a tendency to group about in the sociable area of the cookers where they stood, dropping brief words in confirmation of the narratives of the garrulous few, weary to exhaustion, eager for food and for rest, but for the while content with the negative joys of being merely out of it.

"It is now that are told stories that will perhaps never be told again, for on his return from the line slowly but surely the civilian habit of mind reasserts itself, standards that are based on the sanctity of human life and which are at variance with the grim necessities of the hop-over, assume their normal control. I assume that in many cases good soldiers will no more talk in the decencies of civil life of things they have had to do in war than they will practise them there. . . ."

Lightly Wounded at a Menin Road Dressing Station

". . . . A brush had been passed over all the faces of these wounded, wiping out differences of expression, of character and intelligence; leaving them with something of the facial sameness that we see in different races of a different colour. I suppose it is the suffering and strain, common to them all, which gives them this one-ness of look, the same strain, the same relief, the same apathy, the same unquestioning collapse into the hands of the medicine men."

Stretcher-bearers near Martinpuich

"They move with their stretchers like boats on a slowly tossing sea, rising and falling with the shell riven contours of what was yesterday no man's land, slipping, sliding, with heels worn raw by the downward suck of the Somme mud. Slow and terribly sure through and over everything, like things that have got neither eyes to see terrible things nor ears to heed them . . . . The fountains that sprout roaring at their feet fall back to the earth in a lace-work of fragments—the smoke clears and they, momentarily obscured, are again moving on as they were moving on before: a piece of mechanism guiltless of the weaknesses of weak flesh, one might say. But to say this is to rob their heroism of its due—of the credit that goes to inclinations conquered and panics subdued down in the privacy of the soul. It is to make their heroism look like a thing they find easy. No man of woman born could find it that. These men and all the men precipitated into the liquescent world of the line are not heroes from choice—they are heroes because someone has got to be heroic. It is to add insult to the injury of this world war to say that the men fighting it find it agreeable or go into it with light hearts."

"Waiting for the Stew"

". . . . A dixie of stew for each company was to arrive with the machine guns at the pill box at 12.30 and then into the line. But there was a block on the corduroy—Fritz was putting salvoes onto the road and the cookers could not get past the jam at ——, so the dixies were man-handled from there across the duckboards where duckboards were and across the mud where they were not to the pill box. They arrived there at three o'clock. During the wait the innocent 'J——,' the Mule King, the Prince of the Packs, was roundly consigned to many kinds of torment, the dreadful possibility of going in without that stew began to haunt the strongest and the bravest. . . . . It was a process of sitting still in the dripping cover of that triumph of German architecture, Sexton House, and watching the appetite grow, assisted by some blood-curdling comments of the Doc's."

In the Tunnel—Hill 60

". . . . the companies staging in the tunnels were resting in every conceivable attitude of weariness in slush that was everywhere, and everywhere rising higher. The circumstances were bearable to what they would be in the line, but fatigue even here, to the unlucky forced to spend a night in the bad spots of the tunnels, is a circumstance the aching misery of which cannot be judged by any standard with which our average civilian is conversant. Fatigue at its worst is to the most articulate of our generation the least familiar of humanity's woes, but here in this world it is about us again with the torturing insistence of the troglodyte past—one of the commonplaces of the Stone Age with which war and the wonders of science have familiarised us. . . . The brutish weariness of our earliest hairy forbear, trembling in the savage morasses of an unfamiliar planet, is the daily lot of men like these—shopmen, men from the forge and factory and mine—heirs to all the amenities of the ages. It is part of the supremacy in suffering of the inarticulate infantry. Fatigue, actual brutish and insensate, is borne by them to a pitch at which mules might be heart-broken. Dull, undecorative heroism it is—that of these men of the 'S——'.

"But the poor fabric of military glory is woven of such—of trials that seem to break down the proud partitions which separate our lot from that of the animals. . . . These heroes of ours, alas, are unsupported by a helpful consciousness of their heroism. That joy is only for the onlooker. The tragic fact is that the incomparable heroisms of this winter warfare bring no compensations to the heroes—no element of dramatic exaltation in the performance of them. They are less swift dramatic acts than long states of siege with exhaustion as the besieger."

Fatalist

". . . . The fatalist is born not made. The growing strain of the game is not producing more fatalists if ducking under shell fire is a proof of an absence of fatalism. For many who never ducked are now ducking, whether from wisdom or war strain they are taking this instinctive precaution. But there is a hardihood that persists through it all—there is a grim fatalist who is not fatalist born but is made it by a sort of savage irritation with the grossly incalculable element in the mischance of death. He does not scorn to duck out of sheer pride—to show he has not the wind up, but because he has his back up. He can't prevent the 'whiz-bangs' and the 'five-nines' but he can defy them. He invests them with a personality, a malignancy of personal enmity directed against himself, . . . and he defies them. As though he were to say, 'If you are going to hit me, you swine, you will hit me, but you can't stop me calling you bastard while you are doing it!'"

Outside the Pill Box

". . . . Men of the Company that had been in occupation of the Pill Box awaiting in no very amiable frame of mind the completion of some detail of the relief . . . . I could not tell what they had to be discontented with in that happy land. Around them was all the pomp and pageantry of war—a landscape the like of which man has never gazed upon since early chaos brooded over all. For Westhoek and Flers—the Somme and the Salient—as they were when they were war areas and it was winter—were landscapes that betrayed to the observant all the material content of war. They were the finished product—the perfection towards which that vast Teutonised industry of war is working. Landscapes without colour as of an evil earth in the throes of its dissolution—an earth torn and mangled with its ghost half given up and hanging over-head like a palpable emanation, half agony, half guilt . . . ."

Coming out at Hill 60

"Little groups of men burdened with the appliances of their trades file slowly across the hummocks of Flanders mud. They come out of endless holes and go into endless holes like lonely ants bent on some ant-like service. . . . . Ant-like in the distance, they loom upon a nearer vision things elemental and Homeric, big with destiny. They are merely soldiers at the base, perhaps shopmen at Brisbane, but they are things of mystery in the line. I feel that here all soldiers of all ranks tend to have the baffling profundity of the peasant, that sense of the nearness to the beginning of things which makes the artist see in the peasant the simple, unsolvable mystery of life reduced to its least common multiple—man shorn of all his vast cultures, which are not mysterious, and left simple man, which is."

"Hanging About"

"One so often sees them—these seemingly purposeless groups, awaiting events with the grim immobility of Sioux braves . . . . doing nothing in places where no man would be for choice. Stretcher bearers they may be, or runners, or a company that has left the sickly foetid odours of the dug outs—reminiscent of fowl houses and tramps in summer—to make room for the relief, and is now standing by in all the taciturn boredom of that condition— silent men whom you pass, with all their taciturnity, with the feeling that they have passed a verdict on you annihilating in its justice. . . . .

"It is men like myself—timid peepers into forbidden places, who look and go, who keep their virginal wonderment at what are the commonplaces of the trenches. And these silent watchers are such a commonplace. . . . Perhaps the men familiar with it are unimpressed by the statuesque quietism of these men in places of risk and great events. . . . with their perpetual air of prisoners innocent and awaiting an unjust sentence. . . . They lounge there awaiting something that will send them into the glare of that limelight again like supers in a tragedy in which the supers are greater tragedians than the heroes."

Down from the Ridge

". . . . and Brigades of the —— English division came down, fresh from those quagmires in front of Passchaendael. Officers and men, they were in the last stage of exhaustion—in that condition where every forward step is a battleground on which the desire not to take it has to be met and conquered before that step is taken. They had foot slogged it all the way from C——. W——., and had only stayed there an hour—they looked what they were, men really dead but that their hearts would not let them lie down and die . . . . They spoke with that level exhausted voice of overdone men—if they spoke at all . . . . The little subaltern to whom we told the distance to S——, groaned aloud—but refused the drink we offered—I think it was that he would not allow himself in their extremity something the men could not get . . . . It was a division against which Luck had set its face. Fortune has her favourites among the divisions, and others she pursues with the vindictiveness of an evil step-mother. Every ill circumstance contrivable by collusion between the weather, the enemy, and something we will call Mischance seems to lay in wait for the Brigades upon which the disfavour of Fate has fallen. Poor ——, it was one of them, unlucky on going in, unlucky while in, and unlucky on coming out. . . ."

www.ingramcontent.com/pod-product-compliance
Lightning Source LLC
Chambersburg PA
CBHW070047120526
44589CB00035B/2450